HORSING AROUND

SHOWING HORSES

Creative Education • Creative Paperbacks

Valerie Bodden

Published by Creative Education and Creative Paperbacks
P.O. Box 227, Mankato, Minnesota 56002
Creative Education and Creative Paperbacks are imprints
of The Creative Company
www.thecreativecompany.us

Design and production by Chelsey Luther
Art direction by Christine Vanderbeek
Printed in the United States of America

Photographs by Corbis (David Goldman/AP), Dreamstime (Kseniya Abramova, Anakondasp, Sawitri Khromkrathok, Mikhail Puhachou), iStockphoto (Hedda Gjerpen, KingWu), Shutterstock (Kondrashov Mikhail Evgenevich, Alexia Khruscheva, Charles Knowles, Abramova Kseniya, Anatoliy Lukich, Nightman1965, Jim Noetzel)

Library of Congress Cataloging-in-Publication Data
Bodden, Valerie.
Showing horses / Valerie Bodden.
p. cm. — (Horsing around)
Summary: A narrative guide to showing horses, from how much to practice beforehand, what the show classes entail, what judges are looking for, and what to wear and expect as you perform.
Includes bibliographical references and index.
ISBN 978-1-60818-472-9 (hardcover)
ISBN 978-0-89812-835-2 (pbk)
1. Horses—Showing—Juvenile literature. 2. Show riding—Juvenile literature. I. Title.

SF294.7.B63 2013
798.2'4—dc23 2012049915

HC 9 8 7 6 5 4 3
PBK 9 8 7 6 5 4 3 2

TABLE OF CONTENTS

BEING JUDGED

You ride your horse around the ring. The judges watch as you **trot**. They smile at you when you are finished. You have done well at the horse show!

A horse rider is also called an "equestrian" (*ih-QWEST-tree-en*).

66.9
0.00
ФЕДЕРАЦИЯ
START

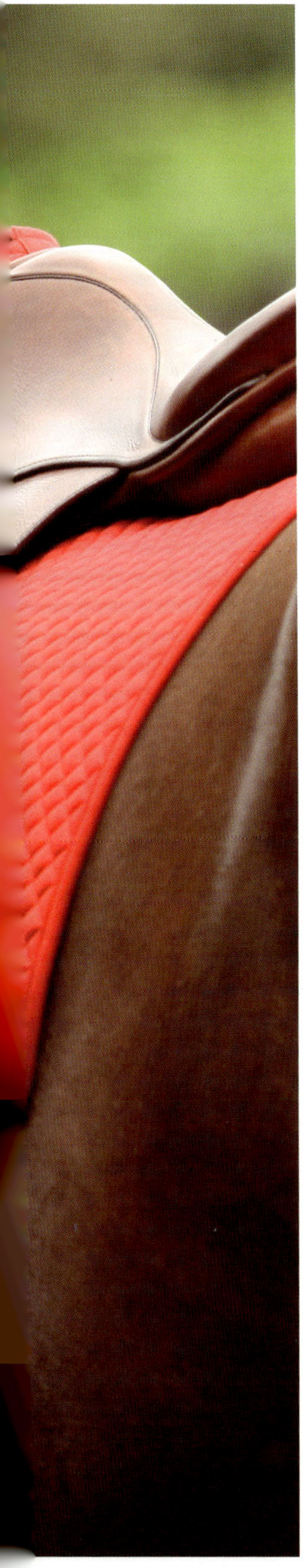

STARTING OUT

BEFORE you can show a horse, you need to go up to it with **confidence**. Touch it lightly on the neck. Talk to it calmly.

A rider can have a strong bond with her horse.

GETTING THERE

You will probably have to travel to get to a horse show. Your horse will ride in a trailer. Horse shows can be outdoors or in an **arena**. You and your horse take part in **classes** at the show.

Some horse trailers are big enough for four horses.

PRACTICE, PRACTICE

You have to practice a lot before being in a horse show. You need to be able to work well with your horse. On the day of the show, you should warm up with your horse.

Warming up helps a horse stretch and get ready.

CLASS ACT

IN some classes, your horse is judged on its walk, trot, and **canter**. The judges watch to see how well the horse follows your commands. In other classes, the judges watch you. They want to see how well you ride and handle your horse.

The equitation class has to do with judging the rider.

Points are given for trying a jump, too.

SHOWY JUMPS

IN the show-jumping class, you ride your horse as it jumps over **rails** or fences. Your ride is usually timed. You get **faults** if your horse knocks down a rail. The horse and rider with the fastest time and fewest faults win.

THE RIGHT MOVES

RIDERS who compete in dressage (*dreh-SAHJ*) make their horses do different types of moves. They make the horse walk and turn. They have it walk sideways or backwards. They even have the horse march in place!

People have trained horses in dressage for hundreds of years.

PIKEUR
236

WHAT TO WEAR

YOU need to look your best for a horse show. Wear riding pants, a shirt, and a riding jacket. You need riding boots and a helmet, too. If you are in a jumping class, wear a **body protector**.

Wearing a body protector helps a rider feel safer.

THE END OF THE DAY

you will find out your score at the end of the class. You might win a ribbon. But the most important thing is that you and your horse had fun working together!

Horses and riders work hard to win at shows.

HORSE DICTIONARY

arena: a large building with lots of space for riding horses

body protector: a thick, hard vest that keeps the chest and back safe during horse jumping events

canter: a way of moving in which a horse keeps the legs on one side of its body in front of the legs on the other side

classes: the different events judged at a horse show, with each class having a winner

confidence: feeling brave and sure, not scared

faults: points given in jumping classes for knocking down a rail, falling off the horse, or taking too long to finish the course

rails: bars going across two posts to form a fence for horses to jump over

trot: a way of moving in which a horse moves the front foot on one side of its body at the same time as the back foot on the other side

READ MORE

De la Bédoyère, Camilla. *Horses and Ponies*. Irvine, Calif.: QEB, 2010.

Pipe, Jim. *Horses*. North Mankato, Minn.: Stargazer Books, 2007.

Ransford, Sandy. *Pony Care*. Irvine, Calif.: QEB, 2011.

WEBSITES

Enchanted Learning: Horse Printout
http://www.enchantedlearning.com/subjects/mammals/horse/Horsecoloring.shtml
Learn more about the parts of a horse, and print a picture of a horse to color.

Olympic.org: Equestrian/Dressage
http://www.olympic.org/videos/equestrian-dressage
Watch videos of dressage from the Olympics.

Every effort has been made to ensure that these sites are suitable for children, that they have educational value, and that they contain no inappropriate material. However, because of the nature of the Internet, it is impossible to guarantee that these sites will remain active indefinitely or that their contents will not be altered.

INDEX